Addition and Subtraction to 20

Key Skills in Maths for ages 5 to 7

Lynne Burgess

For Key Stage 1 of the National Curriculum in England and Wales, and Northern Ireland; and towards Level A of Mathematics 5-14 in Scotland.

HEINEMANN

Heinemann Educational Publishers
Halley Court, Jordan Hill, Oxford OX2 8EJ
a division of Reed Educational & Professional Publishing Ltd

MELBOURNE AUCKLAND
FLORENCE PRAGUE MADRID ATHENS
SINGAPORE TOKYO SAO PAULO
CHICAGO PORTSMOUTH (NH) MEXICO
IBADAN GABORONE JOHANNESBURG
KAMPALA NAIROBI

© Heinemann Educational 1995

Copyright notice
Copies may be made of the sheets in this pack provided that the pack has been paid for and such copies are used solely within the institution for which the pack is purchased. Material sent on approval or inspection and not yet paid for may not under any circumstances be copied. For copying in any other circumstances (e.g. by an external resource centre) prior permission must be obtained from the publisher and a fee may be payable.

ISBN 0 435 02342 X (single title)
ISBN 0 435 02348 9 (omnibus pack)
00 99 98
10 9 8 7 6 5 4

Designed and typeset by StoreyBooks

Illustrated by Rachel Conner

Cover design by The Point

Printed and bound in Great Britain by Thomson Litho Ltd, East Kilbride, Scotland

Contents

Addition within 10

Towards level 1/Level A
1	Seaside	Addition to 5
2	Sand castles	Addition facts for 5
3	Fishing	Addition facts for 6
4	Slides	Addition facts for 10
5	Frog game	Counting on

Towards Level 2
6	Snowmen	Addition to 5
7	Sledges	Addition to 10

Subtraction within 10

Towards Level 1
8	Cakes	Subtraction to 5
9	Climbing	Subtraction facts for 5
10	Christmas presents	Subtraction to 10
11	Snails game	Counting back

Towards Level 2
12	Rabbits	Subtraction to 5
13	Woodlice	Subtraction to 10

Mixed addition and subtraction

Towards Level 1
14	Crackers	Link between + and –

Towards Level 2
15	Windmill	Mixed + and – to 5
16	Bubbles	Facts for 4 and 5
17	Sharks	Facts for 8 and 9
18	Flying kite	Facts to 10
19	Treasure	Counting on and back
20	Pirates	Story problems
21	Wizard	Missing numbers
22	Magic	Missing signs

Addition and subtraction within 20

Towards Level 3/ Level B
23	Jack and Jill	Addition to 20
24	Hickory Dickory Dock	Addition to 20
25	Ladybirds	Subtraction to 20
26	Spider game	Subtraction to 20
27	Packing toffees	Function machines: +10, –5
28	Cherry machine	Function machines: doubles

Introduction

The Key Skills series provides attractive and varied photocopiable sheets to extend and supplement core schemes and other resources. The up-to-date content fits National Curriculum requirements and Mathematics 5–14 in Scotland, and covers a range of work appropriate from Reception to Year 2. Its blend of traditional and more open activities will help children improve their maths skills while discovering that maths can be fun.

The books have been designed for the busy teacher: quick and easy access to mathematical content, and simply worded sheets requiring minimal teacher intervention. The photocopiable format allows flexibility to differentiate between the needs of individual children. Although there is progression between worksheets, not every child will need to complete each sheet, whereas some children may need further practical activities before attempting a sheet.

It is important to ensure children understand the task before they begin, by discussing each sheet with them. Any equipment required is indicated at the top of the page, otherwise just pencils and colouring media are needed. For particular sheets, some children may benefit from the support of extra practical apparatus, such as counting aids.

It is important for children to talk about their mathematical activities. Sometimes discussion may be more valuable while the child is working and sometimes after a sheet has been completed. Help the children identify when it would be appropriate for them to discuss their work with others: a friend, an older child, small group or class helper, and encourage them to share their enthusiasm in what they are learning with parents.

Name _____

Seaside

Fill in the number sentences.

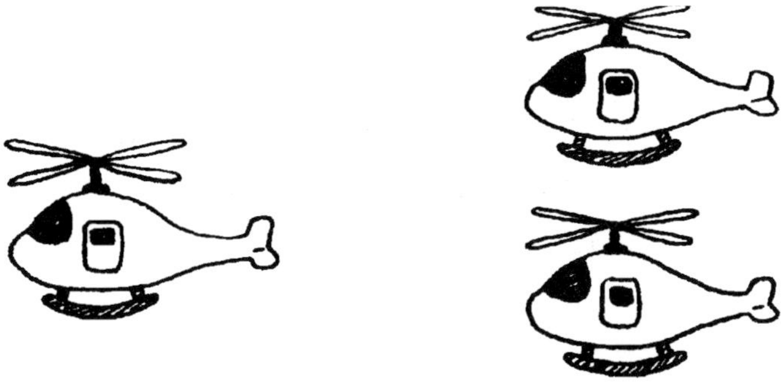

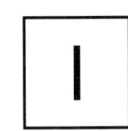

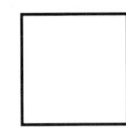

| 1 | + | ☐ | = | ☐ |

☐ + ☐ = ☐

☐ + ☐ = ☐

☐ + ☐ = ☐

Addition to 5

© Heinemann Educational 1995. Restricted copyright cleared.

Name _____

Sand castles

Draw 5 flags on the towers of each sand castle.
Make each sand castle different.

⬜ 1 ⬛ + ⬜ 4 ⬛ = ⬜ 5 ⬛

⬜ + ⬜ = ⬜ 5 ⬛

⬜ + ⬜ = ⬜

⬜ + ⬜ = ⬜

⬜ + ⬜ = ⬜

⬜ + ⬜ = ⬜

Addition facts for 5 © Heinemann Educational 1995. Restricted copyright cleared.

Name _____

Fishing

3

Draw 6 fish in each pair of nets. Make each pair different.

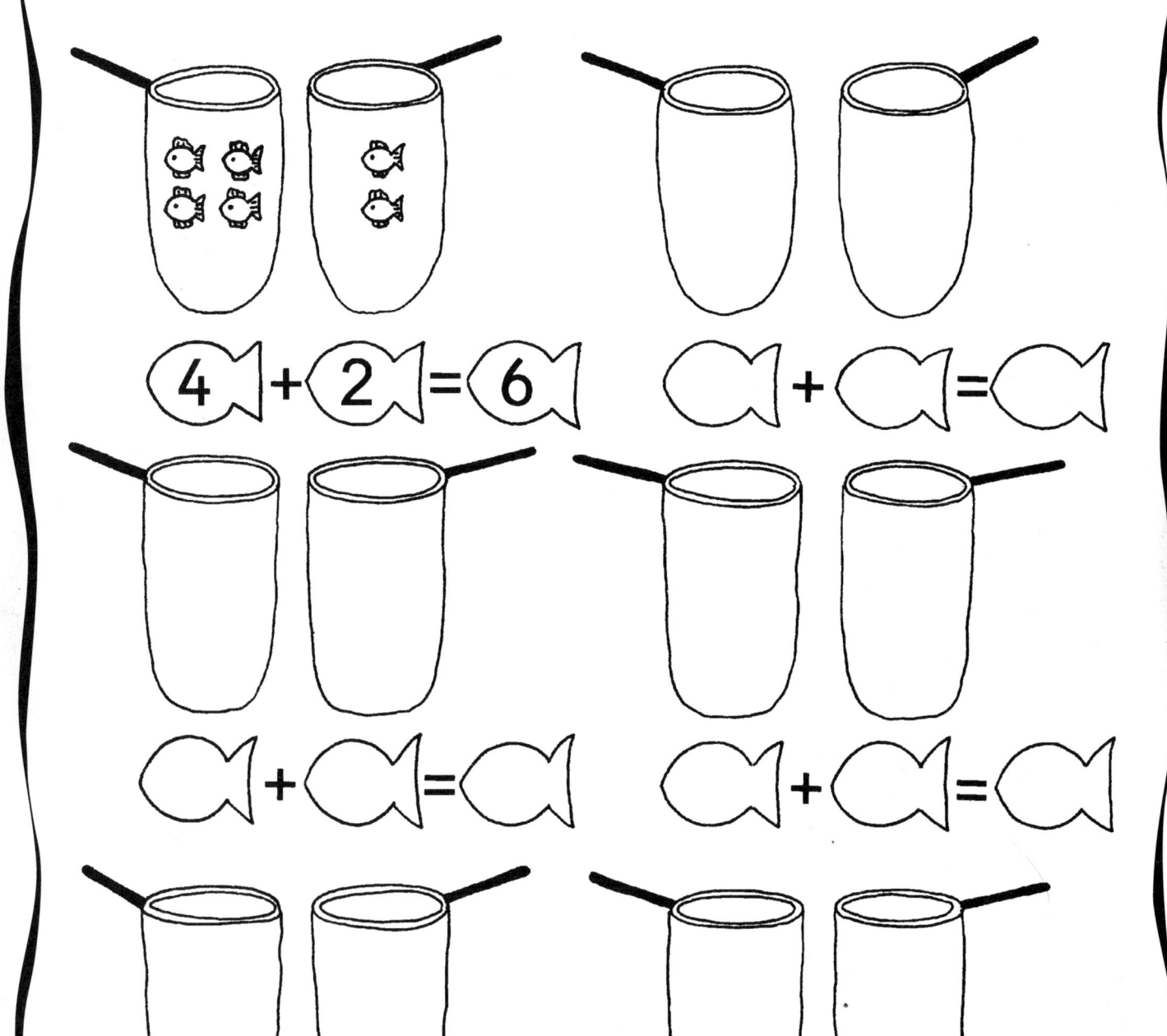

4 + 2 = 6

☐ + ☐ = ☐

☐ + ☐ = ☐

☐ + ☐ = ☐

☐ + ☐ = ☐

☐ + ☐ = ☐

Addition facts for 6

© Heinemann Educational 1995. Restricted copyright cleared.

Name _____

4

Slides

Use 2 colours to colour each slide. Make each slide different.

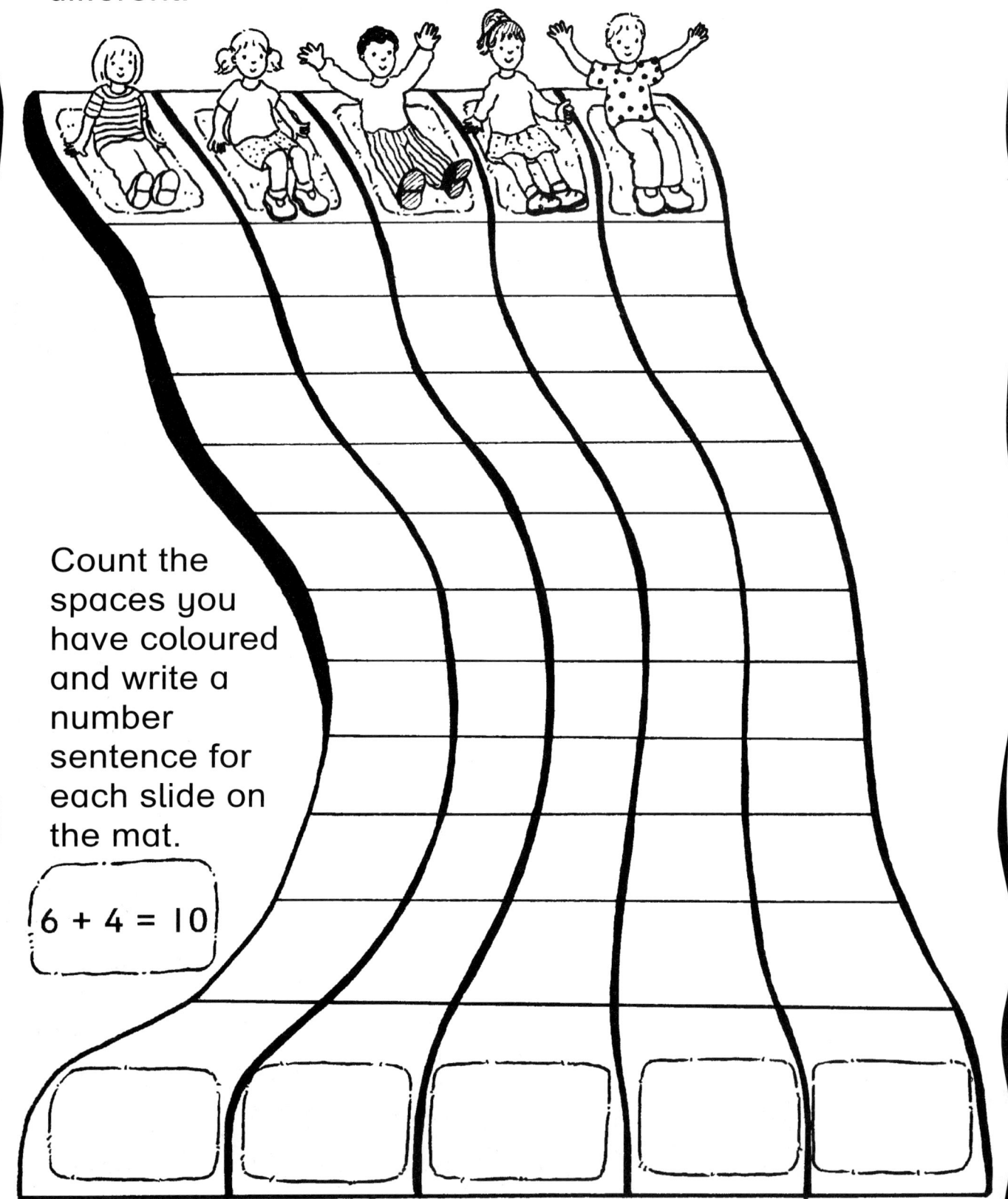

Count the spaces you have coloured and write a number sentence for each slide on the mat.

6 + 4 = 10

Addition facts for 10

© Heinemann Educational 1995. Restricted copyright cleared.

Name _____

Frog game

5

Play with a friend. Use a sheet each. Take turns to throw the dice and jump your frog along the stones. Colour each stone your frog stops on.

Start

jump on 2

jump on 1

jump on 4

jump on 3

jump on 2

jump on 4

jump on 6

Who got to the pond first? _____

Counting on

© Heinemann Educational 1995. Restricted copyright cleared.

Name _____

6

Snowmen

Colour the snowmen with numbers that make 5.

Addition to 5

© Heinemann Educational 1995. Restricted copyright cleared.

Sledges

Name _____

7

Add the numbers on each sledge and match to a child wearing that number.

- 7 + 2
- 5 + 3
- 1 + 6
- 5 + 5
- 6 + 3
- 4 + 4
- 4 + 2
- 2 + 3

Children wearing: 7, 10, 9, 8, 9, 8, 5, 6

Addition to 10

© Heinemann Educational 1995. Restricted copyright cleared.

Name _____

8

Cakes

Draw flames to show the candles left alight.

How many left alight?

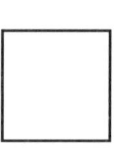

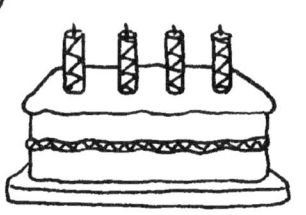

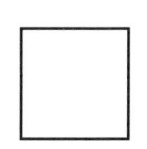

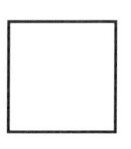

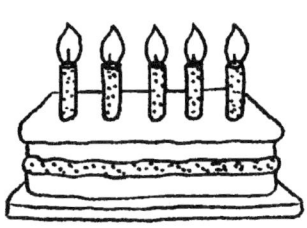

I blow out 1

I blow out 2

I blow out 1

I blow out 3

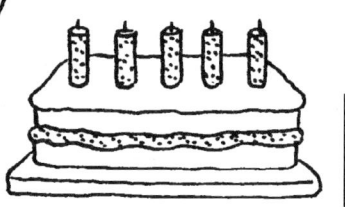

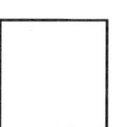

Draw candles of your own.

I blow out _____

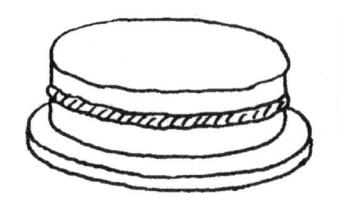

Subtraction to 5

© Heinemann Educational 1995. Restricted copyright cleared.

Name _____

9

Climbing

Use counters to show 5 children on the climbing frame.

Some children get off. Write take away number sentences about them. Make each one different.

5 − 0 = 5

5 − □ = □

5 − □ = □   5 − □ = □

5 − □ = □   5 − □ = □

Subtraction facts for 5   © Heinemann Educational 1995. Restricted copyright cleared.

Name _____

Christmas presents

Draw the presents left in the stockings.

How many left?

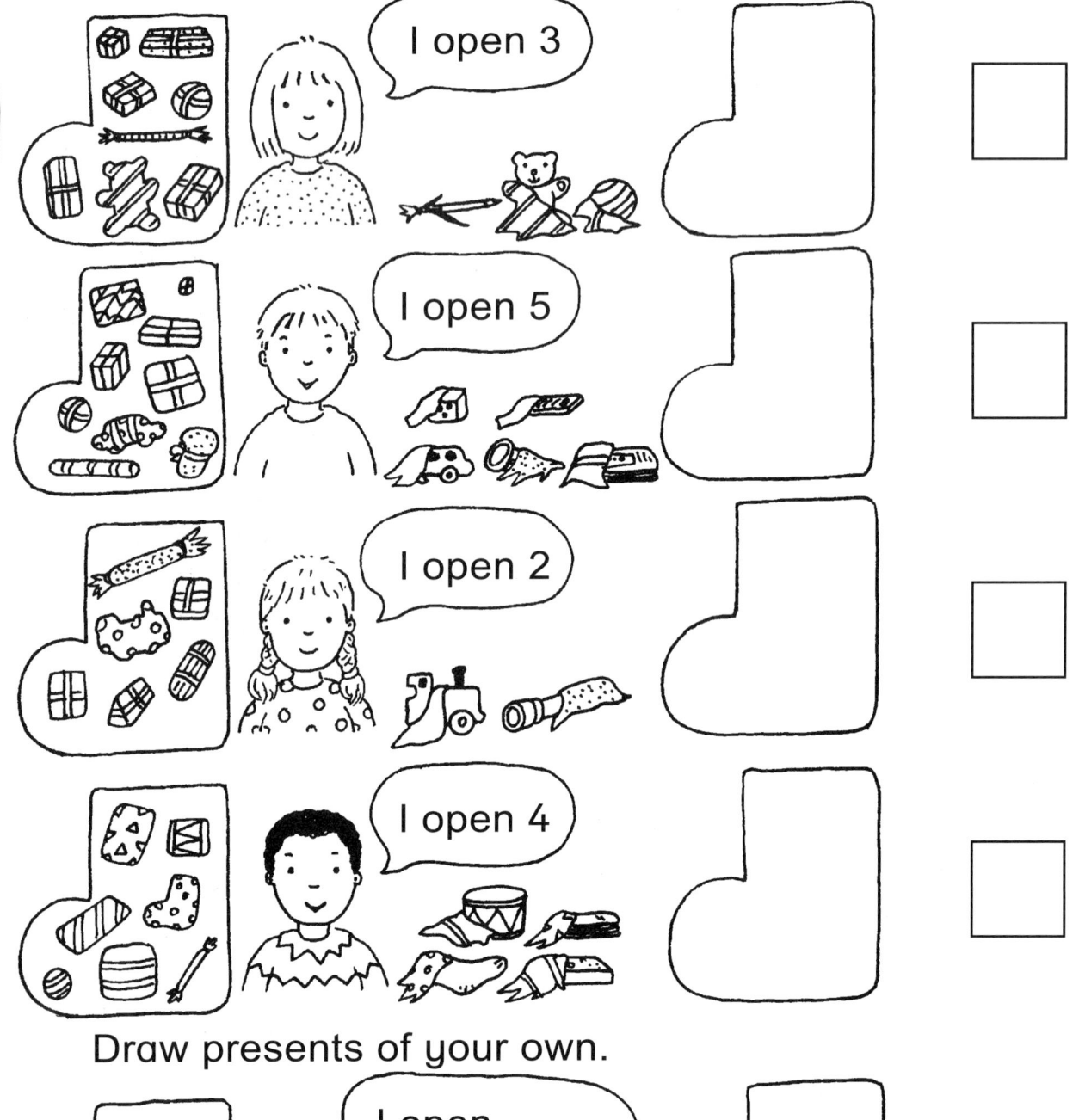

I open 3

I open 5

I open 2

I open 4

Draw presents of your own.

I open ____

Subtraction to 10

© Heinemann Educational 1995. Restricted copyright cleared.

Name _____

Snails game

Play with a friend. Use a sheet each. Take turns to throw the dice and slide your snail up the stalk. Colour each square your snail stops on.

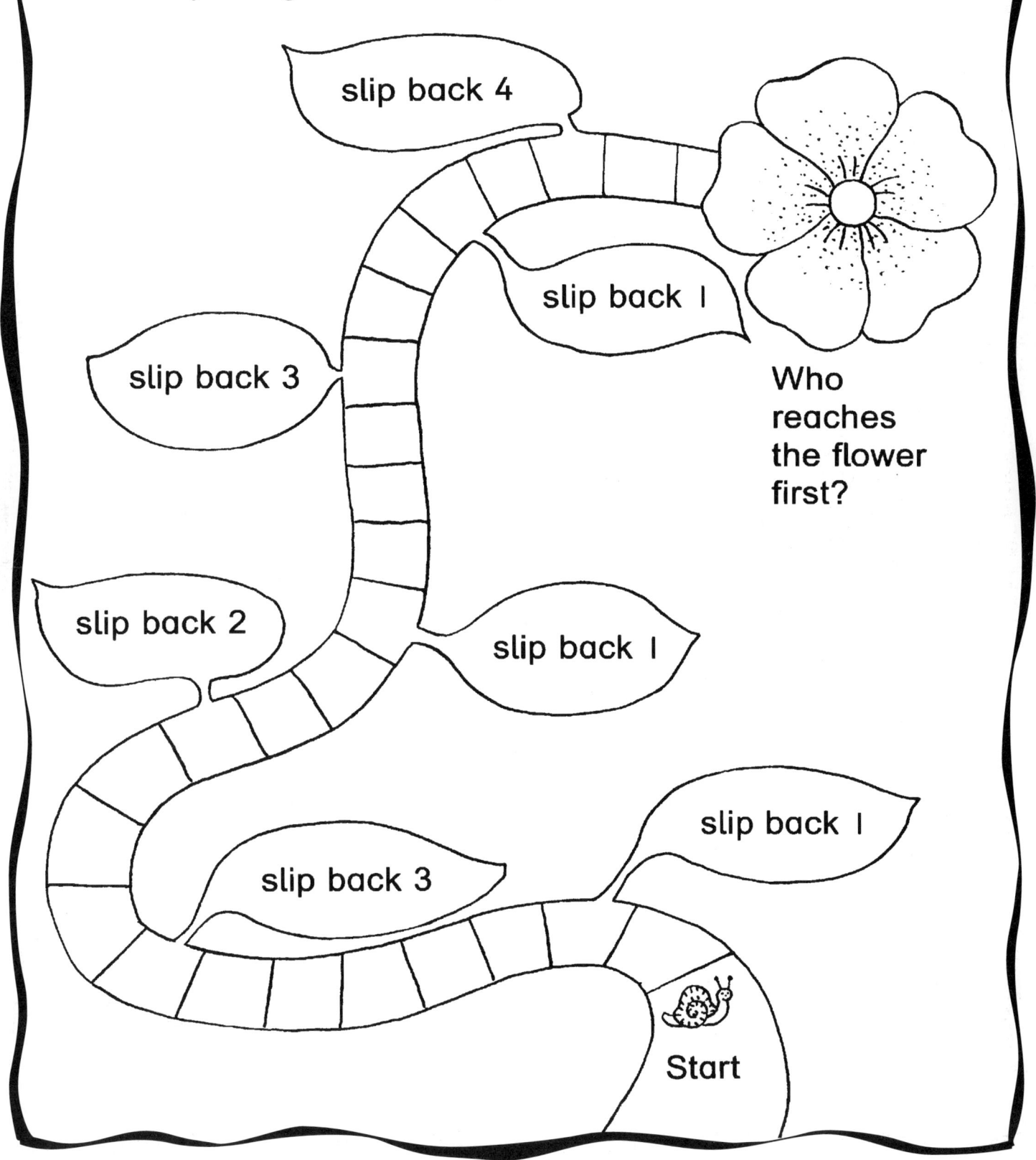

slip back 4

slip back 1

Who reaches the flower first?

slip back 3

slip back 2

slip back 1

slip back 1

slip back 3

Start

Counting back

Name _____

12

Rabbits

This rabbit eats carrots whose answers are 3.
Colour the carrots he can eat.

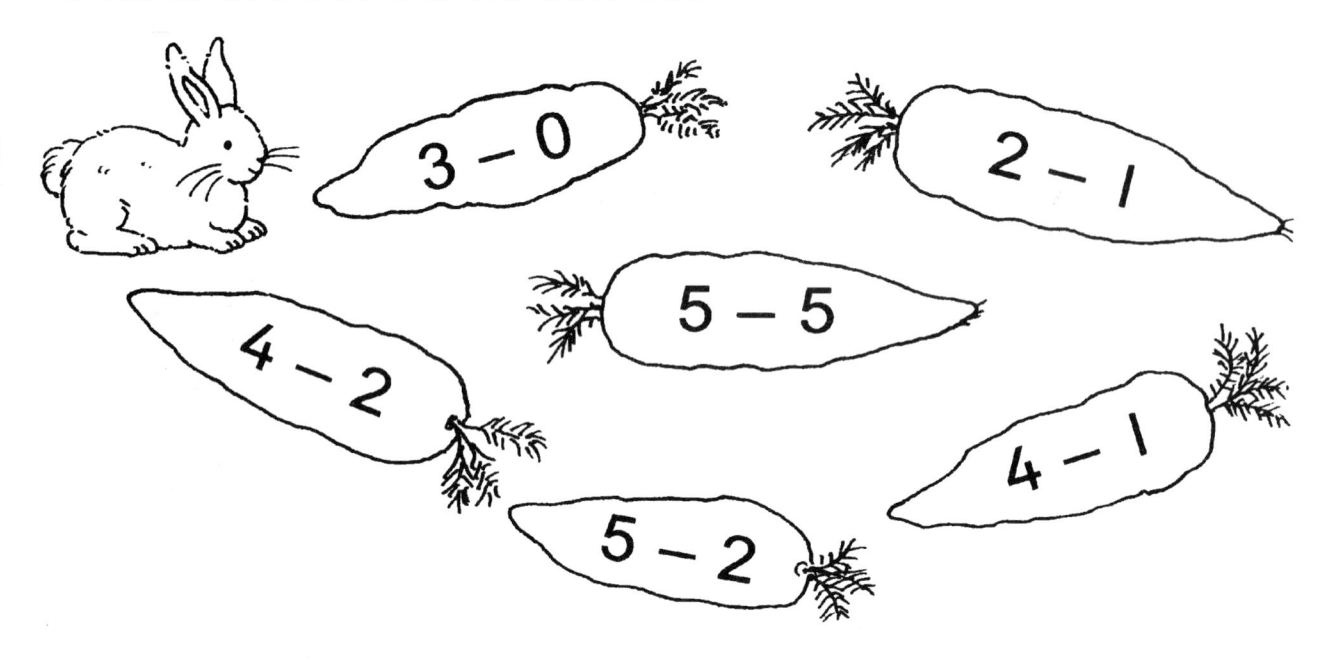

3 − 0
2 − 1
5 − 5
4 − 2
4 − 1
5 − 2

This rabbit eats carrots whose answers are 1.
Write some for him to eat.

Subtraction to 5

© Heinemann Educational 1995. Restricted copyright cleared.

Woodlice

Woodlice like to hide under logs. Match them to their log homes.

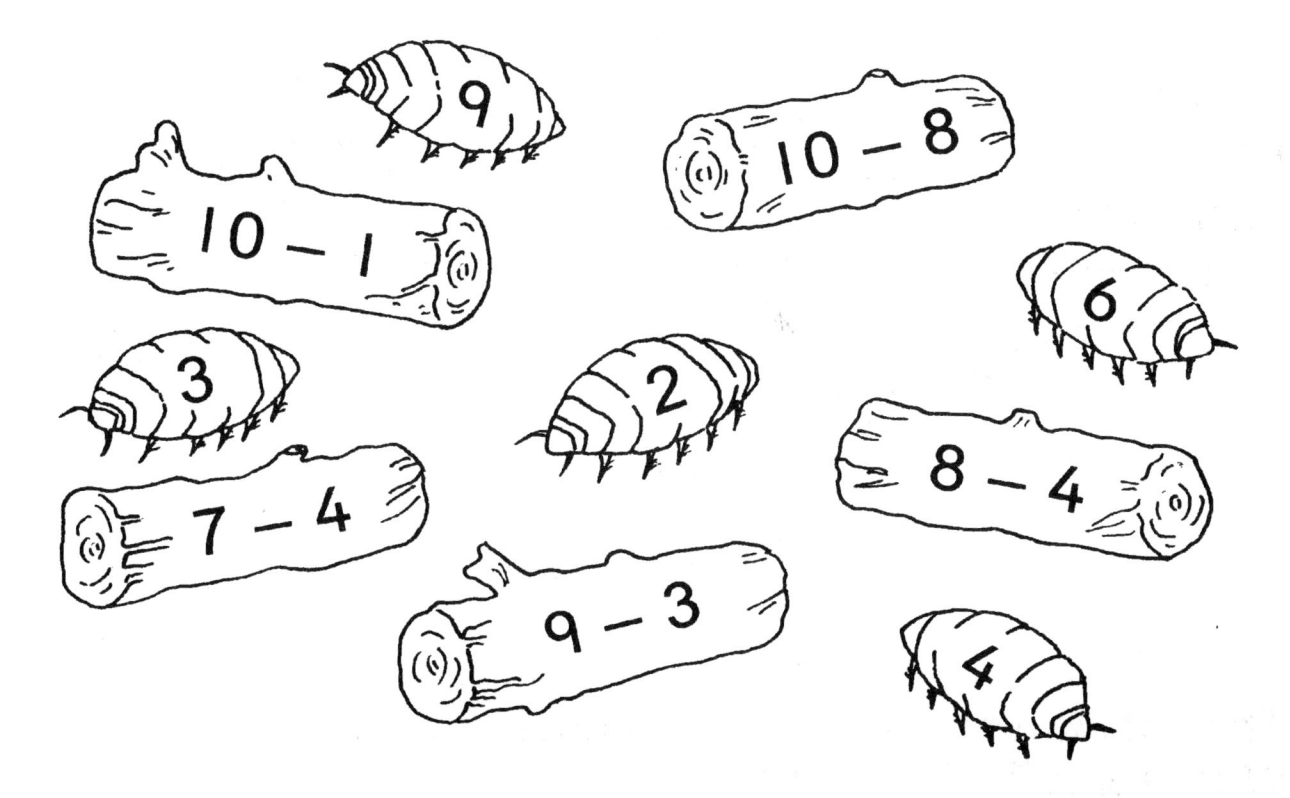

9
10 − 8
10 − 1
6
3
2
8 − 4
7 − 4
9 − 3
4

Write your own numbers and then ask a friend to match.

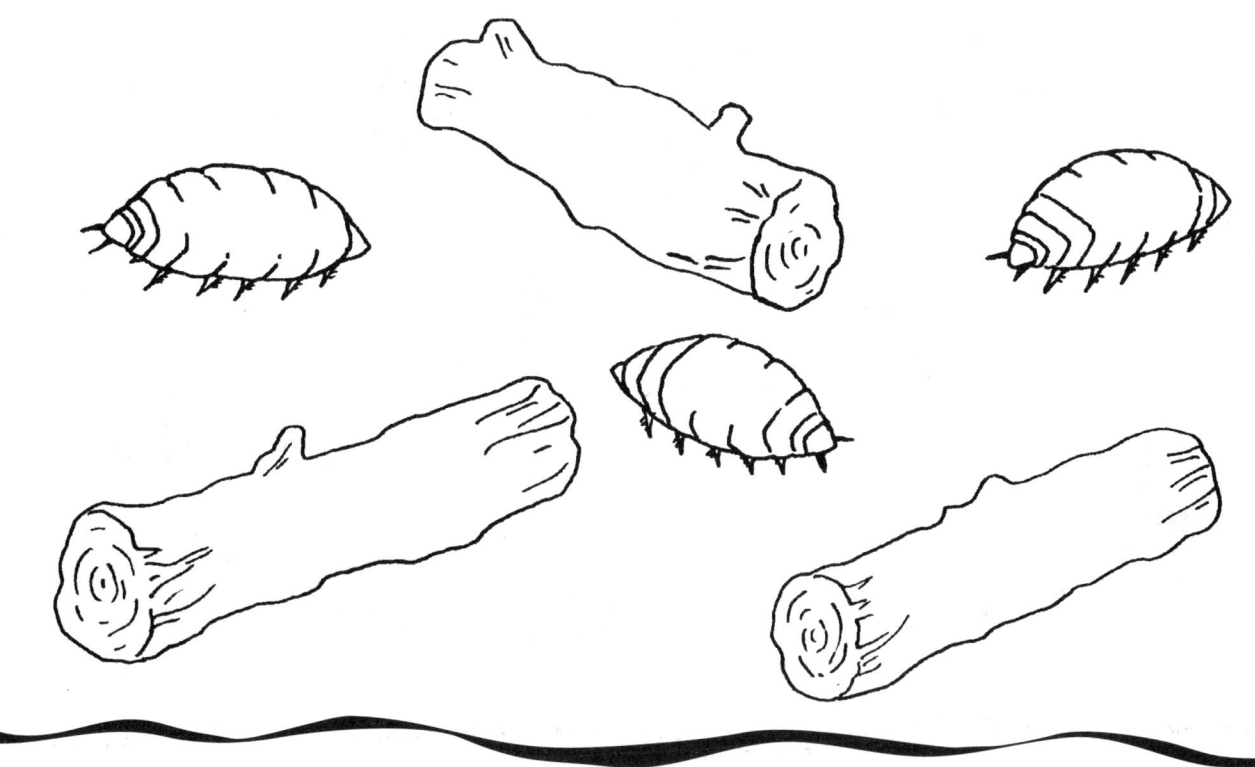

Subtraction to 10

© Heinemann Educational 1995. Restricted copyright cleared.

Name _____

14

Crackers

Write number sentences for each cracker.

3 + 1 =   1 + 3 =

4 − 1 =   4 − 3 =

Link between addition and subtraction   © Heinemann Educational 1995. Restricted copyright cleared.

Name _____

15

Windmill

Write the answer to each number sentence.

4 + 1 =

5 − 0 =

5 − 5 =

3 − 3 =

2 + 2 =

4 − 0 =

2 − 2 =

4 − 4 =

5 − 4 =

4 − 2 =

4 − 3 =

3 − 1 =

3 − 2 =

2 + 0 =

0 + 1 =

Look at your answers.
If the answer is 2, colour the shape green.
If the answer is more than 2, colour the shape blue.
If the answer is less than 2, colour the shape red.

Mixed + and − to 5

© Heinemann Educational 1995. Restricted copyright cleared.

Name _____

Bubbles

16

Write number sentences in the bubbles to match each fish.

1+3

6−2

4

3+2

5

Facts for 4 and 5

© Heinemann Educational 1995. Restricted copyright cleared.

Name _____

Sharks

17

Write number sentences on the fish to match each shark.

8

5 + 4

9

Facts for 8 and 9

© Heinemann Educational 1995. Restricted copyright cleared.

Name _____

Flying kite

Write the answer to each number sentence.

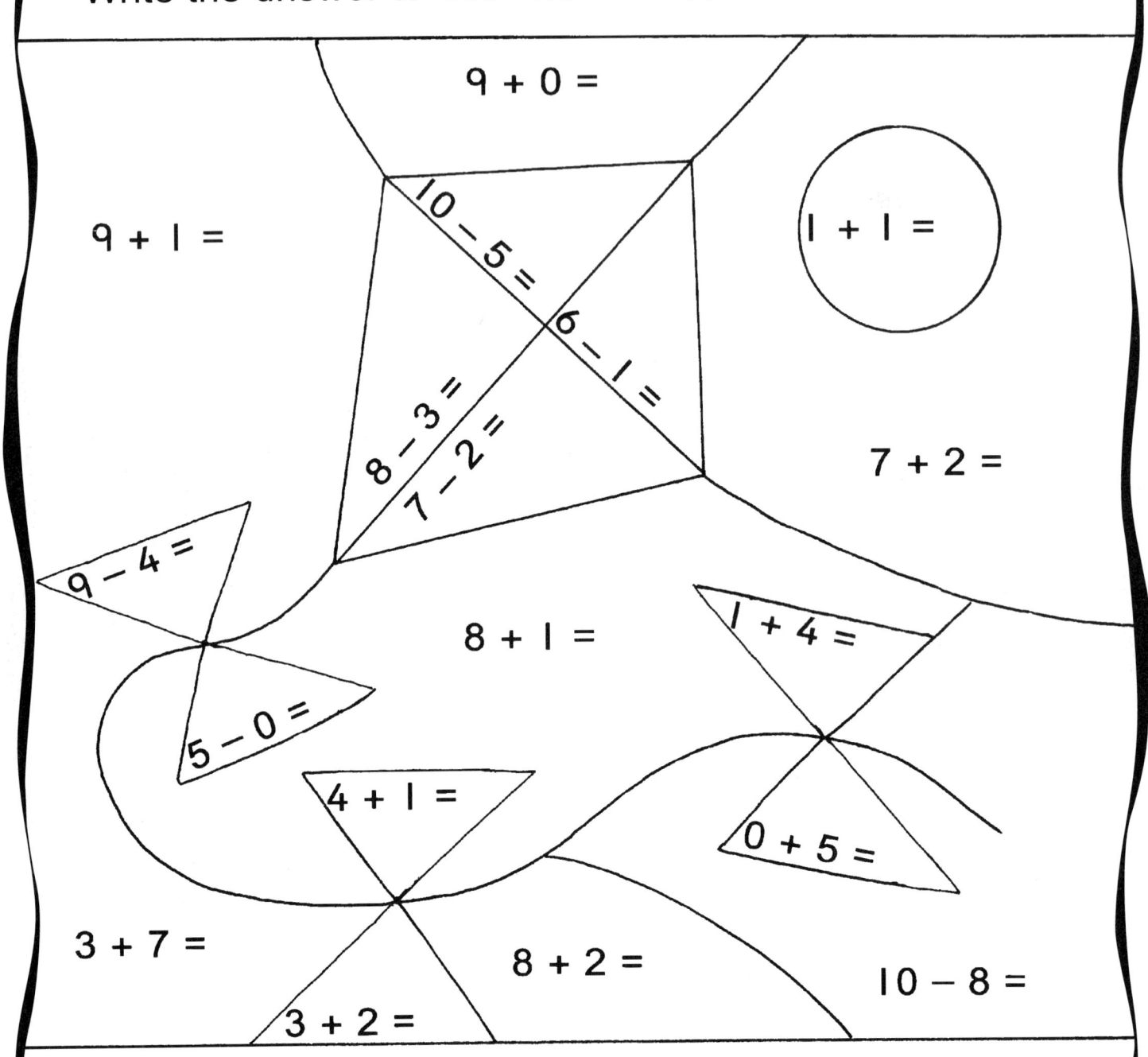

9 + 0 =

9 + 1 =

10 − 5 =

1 + 1 =

8 − 3 =

6 − 1 =

7 − 2 =

7 + 2 =

9 − 4 =

8 + 1 =

1 + 4 =

5 − 0 =

4 + 1 =

0 + 5 =

3 + 7 =

8 + 2 =

10 − 8 =

3 + 2 =

Look at your answers.
If the answer is 5, colour the shape red.
If the answer is more than 5, colour the shape blue.
If the answer is less than 5, colour the shape yellow.

Facts to 10

© Heinemann Educational 1995. Restricted copyright cleared.

Name _____

Treasure

Help the pirates find the treasure. Draw a 🧰 to show where each is hidden.

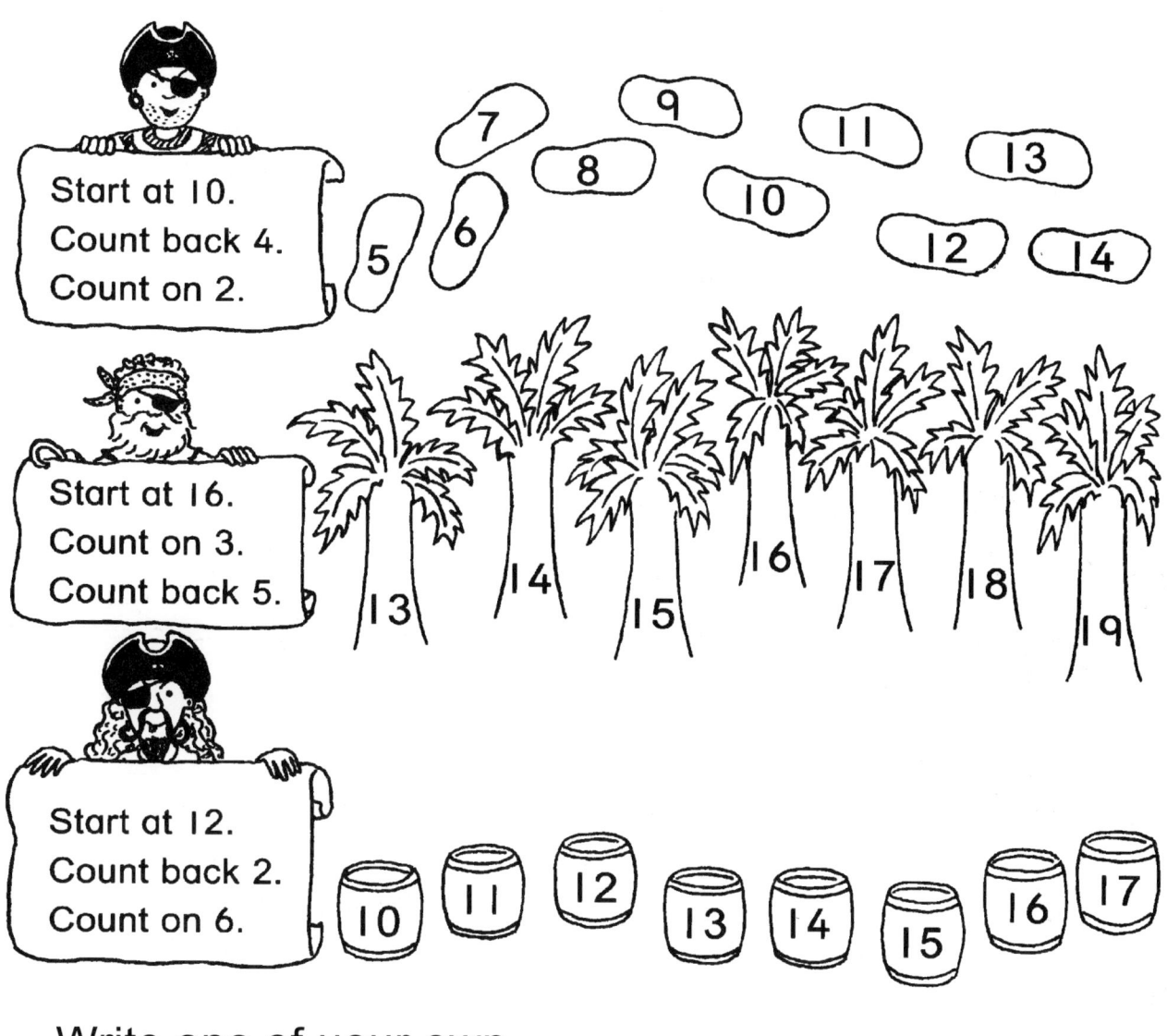

Start at 10.
Count back 4.
Count on 2.

Start at 16.
Count on 3.
Count back 5.

Start at 12.
Count back 2.
Count on 6.

Write one of your own.

Start at
Count back
Count on

Counting on and back

Pirates

20

This pirate has 6 barrels of water.

2 barrels leak. How many left? ☐

He fills 3 more. How many altogether? ☐

4 fall into the sea. How many left? ☐

What happens next? ☐

☐

This pirate has 9 bags of gold.

He finds 1 more. How many altogether? ☐

He drops 2 bags. How many left? ☐

He buys a parrot with 3 bags. How many left? ☐

What happens next? ☐

☐

Story problems

Wizard

Name _____

21

The wizard has made some of the numbers disappear. Write them back in.

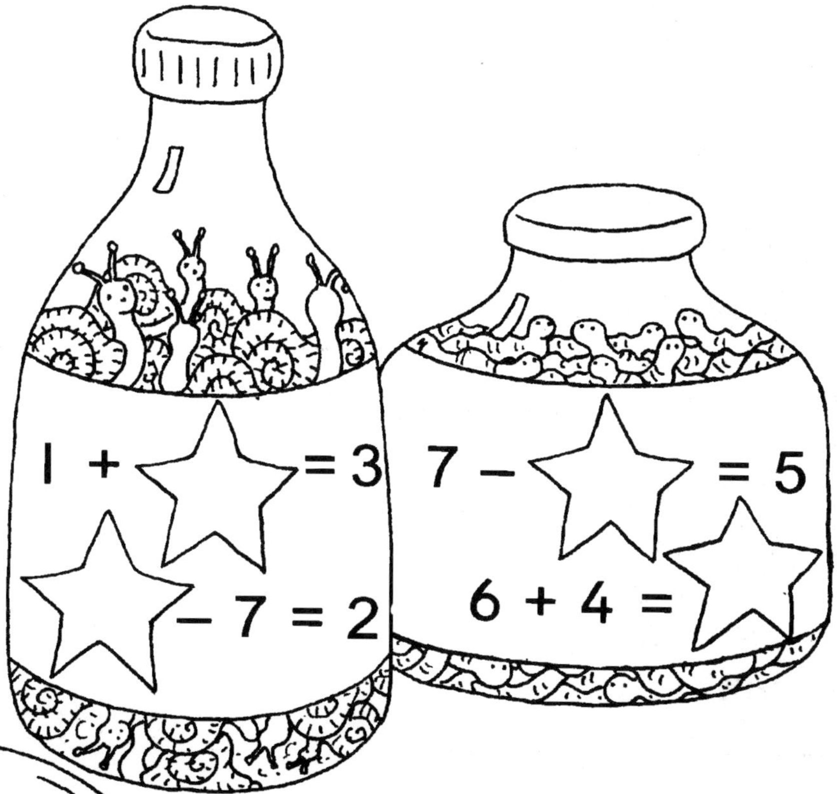

1 + ☆ = 3

☆ − 7 = 2

7 − ☆ = 5

6 + 4 = ☆

10 − ☆ = 9

☆ − 4 = 1

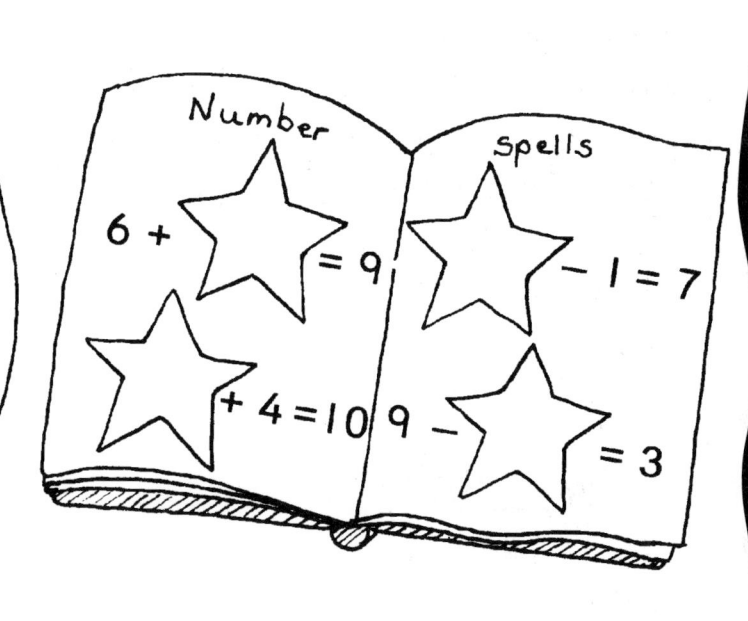

Number spells

6 + ☆ = 9

☆ − 1 = 7

☆ + 4 = 10

9 − ☆ = 3

Missing numbers

© Heinemann Educational 1995. Restricted copyright cleared.

Magic

Name _____

22

The magician has made all the signs disappear.
Write them back in.

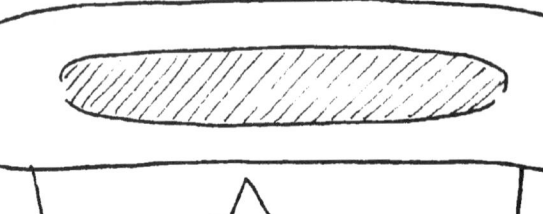

1 ★ 9 = 10

10 ★ 3 = 7

4 ★ 4 = 8

9 ★ 6 = 3

4 ★ 2 = 6

6 ★ 3 = 3

3 ★ 2 = 5

3 ★ 3 = 0

2 ★ 2 = 4

5 ★ 1 = 4

Missing signs

© Heinemann Educational 1995. Restricted copyright cleared.

Name _____

Jack and Jill

Match the buckets to the right well. Colour the buckets which cannot be matched.

23

Well: 12

Buckets: 16+3, 6+6, 15+4, 10+5, 8+4, 11+1, 13+2

Well: 15

Buckets: 14+5, 7+8, 9+3, 17+2, 11+4

Addition to 20

© Heinemann Educational 1995. Restricted copyright cleared.

Name _____

Hickory Dickory Dock

24

20
19
18
17
16
15
14
13
12
11

6 + 5

Write a sum on each cheese to match a number on the clock. Colour the cheese and the number the same.

Addition to 20 © Heinemann Educational 1995. Restricted copyright cleared.

Ladybirds

25

For each ladybird make take away number sentences by colouring pairs of spots. Make each pair a different colour.

Ladybird 1 (head: 15): 20, 16, 18, −1, −3, −5

Ladybird 2 (head: 13): 19, 16, 17, −3, −4, −6

Ladybird 3 (head: 11): 18, 15, 13, −4, −2, −7

Write a take away ladybird of your own and ask a friend to colour it.

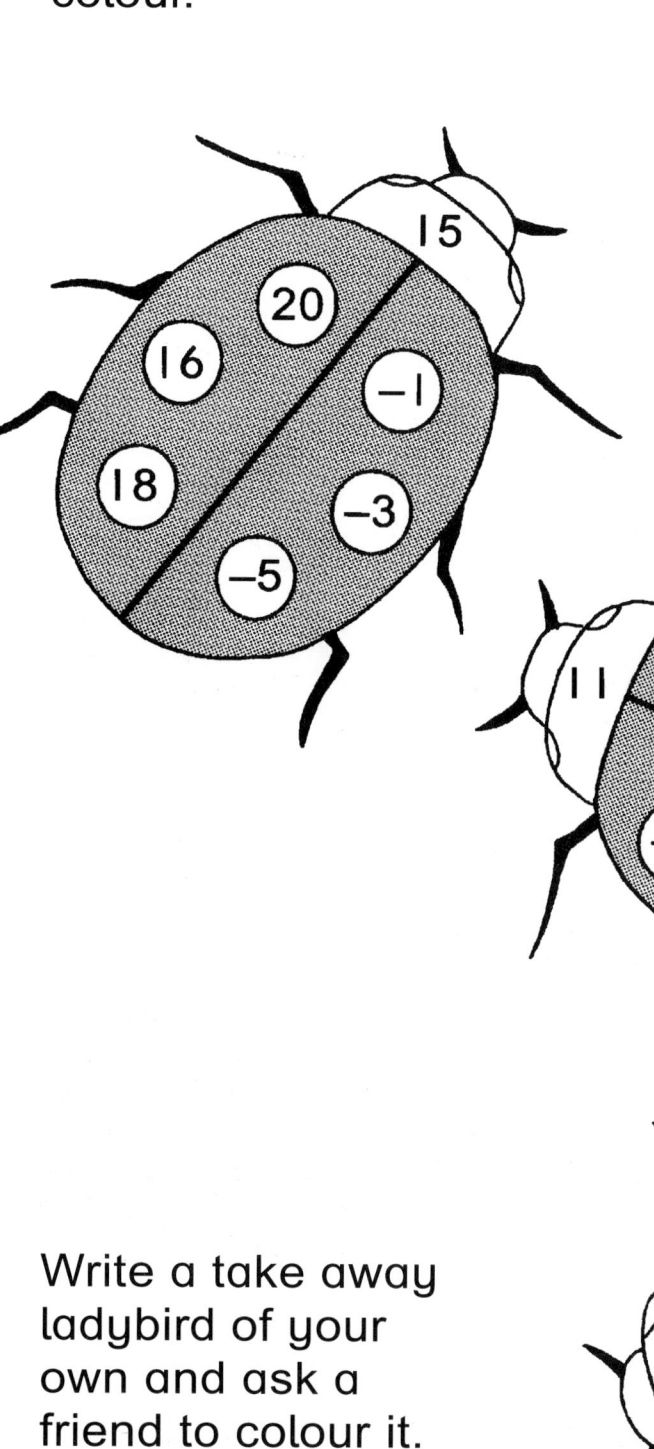

Subtraction to 20

Name _____

Spider game

26

Play with a friend. Use a sheet each and two dice. Take turns to throw the dice. Add the spots and take away from 20. Colour the spider with that number. The winner is the first to colour 6 spiders.

Subtraction to 20 © Heinemann Educational 1995. Restricted copyright cleared.

Packing toffees

Colour the packets red if they have been through the add 10 machine.

Colour them blue if they have been through the take away 5 machine.

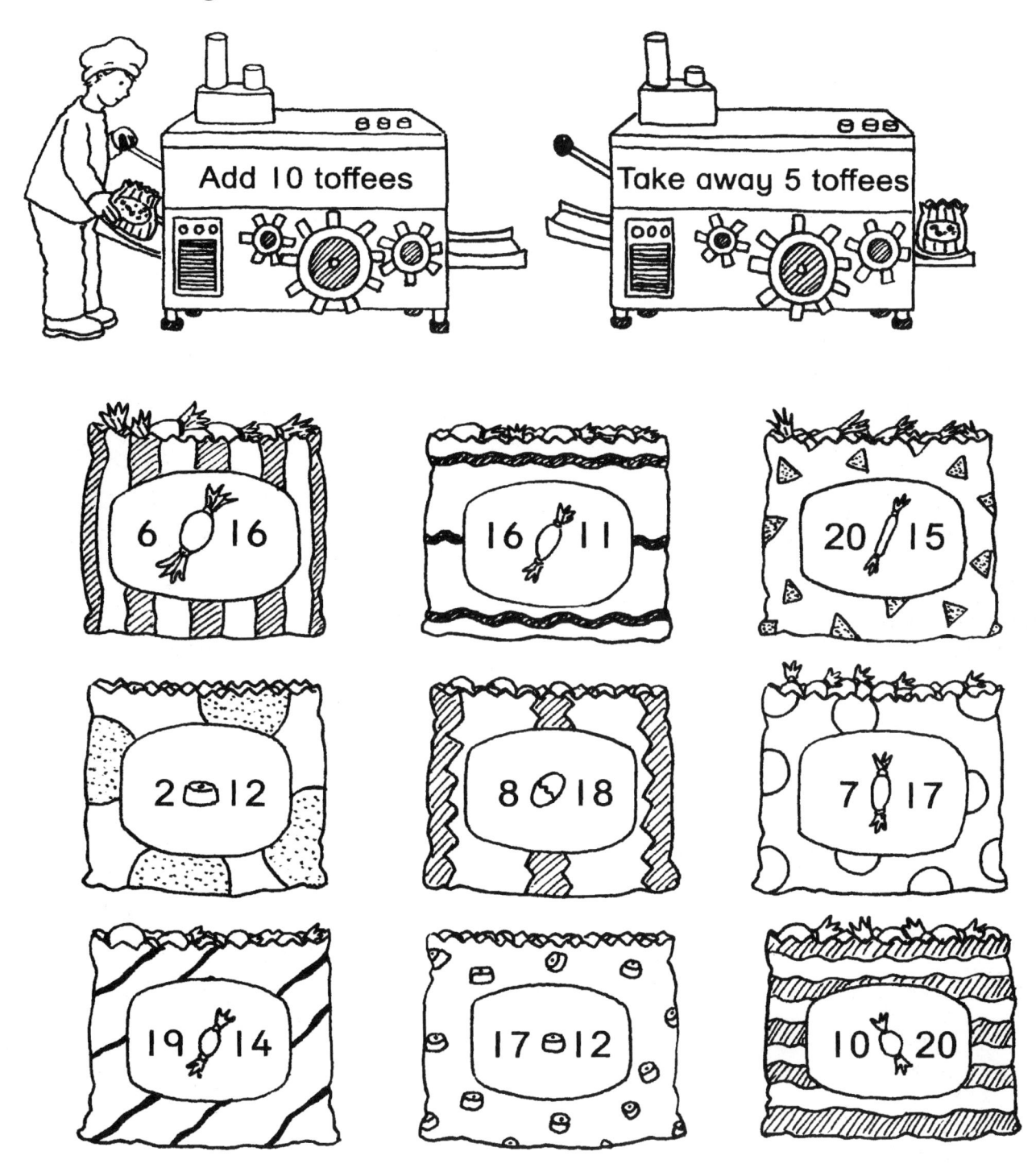

6 → 16	16 → 11	20 → 15
2 → 12	8 → 18	7 → 17
19 → 14	17 → 12	10 → 20

Function machines: +10, −5

Cherry machine

28

Name _____

This machine doubles the number of cherries in each cake. Match the cakes going in the machine to the cakes coming out.

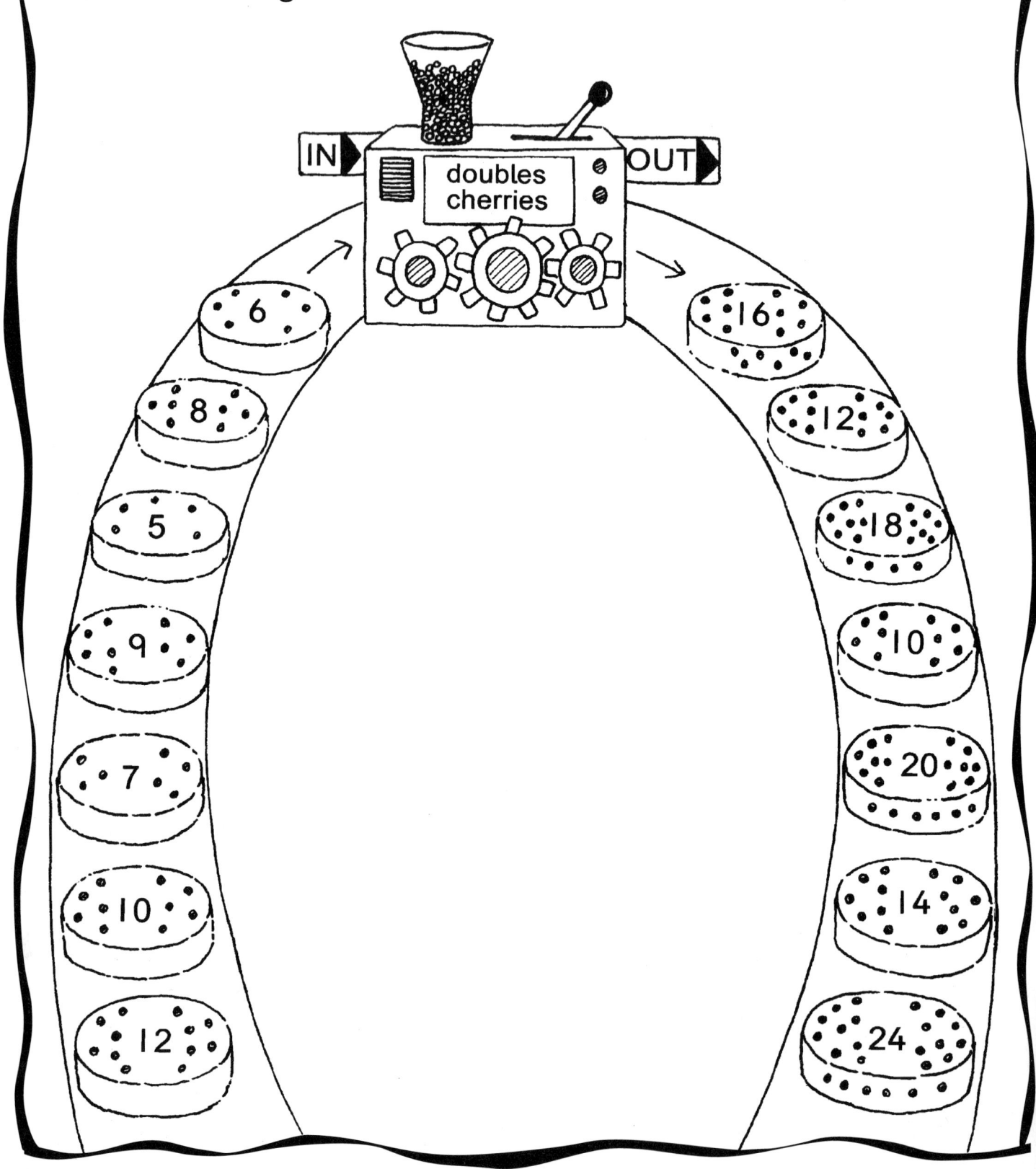

IN ▶   doubles cherries   OUT ▶

In (left side, top to bottom): 6, 8, 5, 9, 7, 10, 12

Out (right side, top to bottom): 16, 12, 18, 10, 20, 14, 24

Function machines: doubles   © Heinemann Educational 1995. Restricted copyright cleared.